THE TEMPEST

Shakespeare The Animated Tales is a multinational venture conceived by S4C, Channel 4 Wales. Produced in Russia, Wales and England, the series has been financed by S4C, the BBC and HIT Communications (UK), Christmas Films and Soyuzmultfilm (Russia), Home Box Office (USA) and Fujisankei (Japan).

Academic Panel
Professor Stanley Wells
Dr Rex Gibson

Academic Co-ordinator
Roy Kendall

Educational Adviser
Michael Marland

Publishing Editor and Co-ordinator
Jane Fior

Book Design
Fiona Macmillan

Animation Director for *The Tempest*
Stanislav Sokolov of Soyuzmultfilm Studios, Moscow

Series Producer and Director
Dave Edwards of The Dave Edwards Studio Ltd, Cardiff

Executive Producers
Christopher Grace
Elizabeth Babakhina

William Heinemann Ltd
Michelin House, 81 Fulham Road
London SW3 6RB
LONDON · MELBOURNE · AUCKLAND
First published 1992
Text and illustrations © Shakespeare Animated Films Limited
and Soyuzmultfilm 1992
ISBN 0 434 96229 5
Printed and bound in the UK by BPCC Hazell Books Limited

The publishers would like to thank Paul Cox for
the use of his illustration of The Globe and
the series logo illustration, Carole Kempe for
her calligraphy, Patrick Spottiswoode for his
introduction and Elizabeth Laird, Ness Wood,
Rosa Fior and Jillian Boothroyd for their help
in the production of the books.

Shakespeare
THE ANIMATED TALES

THE TEMPEST

ABRIDGED BY LEON GARFIELD

ILLUSTRATED BY ELENA LIVANOVA

HEINEMANN YOUNG BOOKS

THE THEATRE IN SHAKESPEARE'S DAY

IN 1989 AN ARCHAEOLOGICAL discovery was made on the south bank of the Thames that sent shivers of delight through the theatre world. A fragment of Shakespeare's own theatre, the Globe, where many of his plays were first performed, had been found.

This discovery has fuelled further interest in how Shakespeare himself conceived and staged his plays. We know a good deal already, and archaeology as well as documentary research will no doubt reveal more, but although we can only speculate on some of the details, we have a good idea of what the Elizabethan theatre-goer saw, heard and smelt when he went to see a play by William Shakespeare at the Globe.

It was an entirely different experience from anything we know today. Modern theatres have roofs to keep out the weather. If it rained on the Globe, forty per cent of the play-goers got wet. Audiences today sit on cushioned seats, and usually (especially if the play is by Shakespeare) watch and listen in respectful silence. In the Globe, the floor of the theatre was packed with a riotous crowd of garlic-reeking apprentices, house servants and artisans, who had each paid a penny to stand for the entire duration of the play, to buy nuts and apples from the food-sellers, to refresh themselves with bottled ale, relieve themselves, perhaps, into buckets by the back wall, to talk, cheer, catcall, clap and hiss if the play did not please them.

In the galleries, that rose in curved tiers around the inside of the building, sat those who could afford to pay two pennies for a seat, and the benefits of a roof over their heads. Here, the middle ranking citizens, the merchants, the sea captains, the clerks from the Inns of Court, would sit crammed into their small eighteen inch space and look down upon the 'groundlings' below. In the 'Lords room', the rich and the great, noblemen and women, courtiers and foreign ambassadors had to pay sixpence each for the relative comfort and luxury of their exclusive position directly above the stage, where they smoked tobacco, and overlooked the rest.

We are used to a stage behind an arch, with wings on either side, from which the actors come on and into which they disappear. In the Globe, the stage was a platform thrusting out into the middle of the floor, and the audience, standing in the central yard, surrounded it on three sides. There were no wings. Three doors at the back of the stage were used for all exits and entrances. These were sometimes covered by a curtain, which could be used as a prop.

Today we sit in a darkened theatre or cinema, and look at a brilliantly lit stage or screen, or we sit at home in a small, private world of our own, watching a luminous television screen. The close-packed, rowdy crowd at the Globe, where the play started at two o'clock in the afternoon, had no artificial light to enhance their illusion. It was the words that moved them. They came to listen, rather than to see.

No dimming lights announced the start of the play. A blast from a trumpet and three sharp knocks warned the audience that the action was about to begin. In the broad daylight, the actor could see the audience as clearly as the audience could see him. He spoke directly to the crowd, and held them with his eyes, following their reactions. He could play up to the raucous laughter that greeted the comical, bawdy scenes, and gauge the emotional response to the higher flights of poetry. Sometimes he even improvised speeches of his own. He was surrounded by, enfolded by his audience.

The stage itself would seem uncompromisingly bare to our eyes. There was no scenery. No painted backdrops suggested a forest, or a castle, or the sumptuous interior of a palace. Shakespeare painted the scenery with his words, and the imagination of the audience did the rest.

Props were brought onto the stage only when they were essential for the action. A bed would be carried on when a character needed to lie on it. A throne would be let down from above when a king needed to sit on it. Torches and lanterns would suggest that it was dark, but the main burden of persuading an audience, at three o'clock in the afternoon, that it was in fact the middle of the night, fell upon the language.

In *The Tempest*, Shakespeare has to go a step further and make the audience experience a violent storm at sea. Voices shout 'We split! We split!' and 'Hell is empty and all the devils are here!'

Shakespeare's actors were responsible for their own costumes. They would use what was to hand in the 'tiring house' (dressing room), or supplement it out of their own pockets. Classical, medieval and Tudor clothes

The curtain rises on Prospero's isle, a strange, uninhabited place, mysterious with mists, and set in the midst of a glassy sea. The lord of the isle, clad in his magic mantle, stands upon a promontory with his arm about his daughter, Miranda. Together, they gaze out towards a distant ship. Prospero's eyes are glittering.

At last, after twelve long years on the haunted isle, his enemies are within his grasp: his wicked brother Antonio, Alonso, the greedy King of Naples, and his treacherous brother Sebastian; even Gonzalo, the kindly courtier who, when he and his tiny daughter had been set adrift in a rotting boat, had secretly provided them with food and clothing, and those precious books from his library that had turned the poor, betrayed Duke of Milan into Prospero, the mighty enchanter.

He raises the carved staff he holds in his right hand, and stretches out towards the distant ship. At once, a black cloud appears in the clear sky. It assumes a wild and savage shape, and pounces on the vessel. It is full of dazzling worms of lightning, and the vessel heaves and twists in a vain effort to escape. Tiny shouts and screams reach the silent onlookers.

VOICES	We split, we split!
A VOICE	Hell is empty and all the devils are here!

The ship's company leap overboard; then the black cloud obscures all. When it has dispersed, the sea is glassy again. The vessel has vanished.

MIRANDA	Poor souls, they perished!
PROSPERO	Be collected: no more amazement: tell your piteous heart there's no harm done.
MIRANDA	O, woe the day!
PROSPERO	No harm. I have done nothing but in care of thee.

He seats himself; she sits beside him. Fondly, he strokes her hair, then gently touches her eyes.

PROSPERO	Thou art inclined to sleep.

Miranda sleeps. Prospero rises and paces the sands.

PROSPERO	Come away, servant come. I am ready now. Approach, my Ariel, come!

A strange creature manifests itself out of the air, a bright, trembling, vague creature, neither beast nor human, but endlessly changing between them.

ARIEL	All hail, great master! Grave sir, hail!
PROSPERO	Hast thou, spirit, performed to point the tempest that I bade thee?
ARIEL	(*proudly*) To every article! I boarded the King's ship, now on the beak, now in the waist, in every cabin, I flamed amazement!
PROSPERO	My brave spirit!
ARIEL	Not a soul but felt a fever of the mad, and played some tricks of desperation!

PROSPERO	But are they, Ariel, safe?
ARIEL	Not a hair perished! In troops I have dispersed them 'bout the isle. The King's son I have landed by himself.
PROSPERO	Why, that's my spirit! But there's more work—
ARIEL	What, more toil?
PROSPERO	How now? Moody? What is't thou canst demand?
ARIEL	My liberty.
PROSPERO	Before the time be out? No more! Dost thou forget from what a torment I did free thee?
ARIEL	Pardon, master, I will be correspondent to command and do my spiriting gently.
PROSPERO	Do so; and after two days I will discharge thee.

ARIEL   That's my noble master! What shall I do? say what? what shall
          I do?

PROSPERO Go make thyself like a nymph o'the sea, be subject to no sight
          but thine and mine, invisible to every eyeball else. (*Instantly,
          Ariel, with a flurry of strange gestures, becomes a sea-nymph,
          lovely and delicate.*) Fine apparition! My quaint Ariel, hark in
          thine ear. (*He whispers in Ariel's ear*).

ARIEL   My lord, it shall be done. (*He vanishes.*)

Prospero returns to the sleeping Miranda.

PROSPERO Awake, dear heart, awake! Thou hast slept well. (*Miranda
          wakes.*) Come on, we'll visit Caliban, my slave—

MIRANDA   'Tis a villain, sir, I do not love to look on.

PROSPERO But as 'tis we cannot miss him: he does make our fire, fetch in
          our wood. (*Together, they walk to the entrance of a cave.*)
          What, ho! Slave! Caliban! Thou earth, thou! Come forth!

*With much groaning, Caliban, a monstrous, deformed crea-
ture, crawls out.*

CALIBAN   A south-west blow on ye and blister you all o'er!

PROSPERO For this, be sure, tonight thou shalt have cramps, side-stitches
          that shall pen thy breath up—

CALIBAN I must eat my dinner. This island's mine, by Sycorax my mother, which thou tak'st from me. When thou cam'st first, thou strok'st me and made much of me, would'st give me water with berries in't, and teach me how to name the bigger light, and how the less, that burn by day and night; and then I loved thee—

PROSPERO Thou most lying slave, whom stripes may move, not kindness! I have used thee, filth as thou art, with human care; and lodged thee in mine own cell, till thou didst seek to violate the honour of my child.

CALIBAN O, ho, O, ho! Would't had been done! Thou did'st prevent me; I had peopled else this isle with Calibans!

PROSPERO Hag-seed, hence! Fetch us in fuel!

CALIBAN (*creeping away*) I must obey. His art is of such power . . .

Another part of the island. The sea-shore. Ferdinand, the king's son, saved from the sea, walks warily. The invisible Ariel leads him with a song:

ARIEL Come unto these yellow sands,
And then take hands:
Curtsied when you have, and kissed,
The wild waves whist . . .

FERDINAND   Where should this music be? I'th'air or th'earth?

ARIEL   Full fathom five thy father lies;
                         Of his bones are coral made;
                         Those are pearls that were his eyes:
                         Nothing of him that doth fade,
                         But doth suffer a sea-change
                         Into something rich and strange . . .

FERDINAND   The ditty does remember my drowned father.

Little by little, the singing, invisible Ariel leads Ferdinand into the presence of Prospero and Miranda.

MIRANDA   What is't? A spirit?

PROSPERO   No, wench; it eats and sleeps and has such senses as we have—such. This gallant which thou seest was in the wreck. He hath lost his fellows and strays about to find 'em.

MIRANDA   I might call him a thing divine; for nothing natural I ever saw so noble!

Even as Miranda stares in wonderment at Ferdinand, so does he stare at the girl.

FERDINAND   Most sure the goddess on whom these airs attend! O you wonder! If you be maid or no?

MIRANDA   No wonder, sir; but certainly a maid.

FERDINAND   My language! heavens! I am the best of them that speak this speech, were I but where 'tis spoken.

PROSPERO   (*aside*) At first sight they have changed eyes! Delicate Ariel, I'll set thee free for this! (*To Ferdinand*) How? the best? What wert thou, if the King of Naples heard thee? A word, good sir, I fear you have done yourself some wrong: a word.

MIRANDA   Why speaks my father so ungently? This is the third man that e'er I saw; the first that e'er I sighed for—

FERDINAND   O, if a virgin, and your affection not gone forth, I'll make you the Queen of Naples!

PROSPERO   I charge thee: thou dost here usurp the name thou ow'st not; and hast put thyself upon this island as a spy, to win it from me, the lord on't.

FERDINAND   No, as I am a man!

PROSPERO   (*Miranda moves to defend Ferdinand*) Speak not you for him: he's a traitor. Come, I'll manacle thy neck and feet together—

FERDINAND   No; I will resist—

He draws his sword. Prospero raises his staff, and Ferdinand finds his arm frozen. Desperately, Miranda clutches at her father's mantle.

PROSPERO	Hence! Hang not on my garments!
MIRANDA	Sir, have pity! I'll be his surety!
PROSPERO	What! An advocate for an impostor! Hush! Thou thinkest there is no more shapes such as he, having seen but him and Caliban: foolish wench! To th'most of men this is a Caliban, and they to him are angels.
MIRANDA	My affections are most humble; I have no ambition to see a goodlier man.
PROSPERO	(*to Ferdinand*) Come on, obey!
MIRANDA	Be of comfort; my father's of a better nature, sir, than he appears . . .
PROSPERO	(*aside to Ariel, who has been hovering, invisible*) Thou shalt be as free as mountain winds; but then exactly do all points of my command . . .

A woodland glade, in which the chief survivors of the wreck now find themselves; Alonso, King of Naples; Sebastian, his brother; Antonio, brother to Prospero; Gonzalo, the kindly courtier who had once assisted Prospero and his daughter; and other attending lords. They are plainly weary from walking.

GONZALO	Beseech you, sir, be merry; you have cause, so have we all, of joy; for our escape is much beyond our loss—

ALONSO   Prithee, peace.

SEBASTIAN   (*to Antonio*) He receives comfort like cold porridge.

GONZALO   The air breathes upon us here most sweetly—

SEBASTIAN   As if it had lungs, and rotten ones.

GONZALO   Our garments, being as they were, drenched in the sea, seem now as fresh as when we were at Tunis at the marriage of your daughter who is now Queen.

ALONSO   Would I had never married my daughter there! For, coming thence, my son is lost. O thou mine heir of Naples and Milan, what strange fish hath made his meal on thee?

GONZALO   Sir, he may live; I saw him beat the surges under him—

ALONSO   No, no, he's gone.

SEBASTIAN   Sir, you may thank yourself for this great loss, that would not bless our Europe with your daughter—

ALONSO   Prithee, peace.

SEBASTIAN   The fault's your own!

GONZALO   My lord Sebastian, the truth you speak doth lack some gentleness. You rub the sore when you should bring the plaster.

Ariel appears above, hovering invisibly; and makes strange signs in the air. Gonzalo, the king and the attendant lords become suddenly drowsy. They settle on the ground.

GONZALO   You are . . . gentlemen of—of . . . I am very heavy.

ANTONIO   Go sleep. (*Gonzalo sleeps.*)

ALONSO   I wish mine eyes would, with themselves, shut my thoughts . . . (*He yawns.*) I find they are inclined to do so.

The king sleeps, and following his example so do all, except for Sebastian and Antonio.

SEBASTIAN   What a strange drowsiness possesses them!

ANTONIO   It is the quality o'th'climate.

SEBASTIAN   I find not myself disposed to sleep.

ANTONIO   Nor I.

Antonio glances at the sleeping king, and then looks meaningly at Sebastian.

ANTONIO   What might, worthy Sebastian?—O what might? My strong imagination sees a crown dropping upon thy head.

SEBASTIAN   Prithee, say on.

ANTONIO   Will you grant with me that Ferdinand is drowned?

SEBASTIAN   He's gone.

ANTONIO   Then tell me, who's the next heir to Naples?

SEBASTIAN   Claribel.

THE TEMPEST

ANTONIO   She that is Queen of Tunis; she that dwells ten leagues beyond man's life. (*He nods towards the sleeping king.*) What a sleep were this for your advancement! Do you understand me?

SEBASTIAN   Methinks I do. I remember you did supplant your brother Prospero.

ANTONIO   True: and look how well my garments sit upon me.

SEBASTIAN   Thy case, dear friend, shall be my precedent; as thou got'st Milan, I'll come by Naples. Draw thy sword!

The friends creep upon the sleepers with drawn swords, ready to murder the king and Gonzalo. Swiftly, Ariel descends.

ARIEL   (*in Gonzalo's ear*)Awake, awake!

The sleepers awake, and see Sebastian and Antonio with drawn swords.

ALONSO	Why, how now? Why are you drawn?
GONZALO	What's the matter?
SEBASTIAN	We heard a hollow burst of bellowing, like bulls, or rather lions!
ALONSO	I heard nothing.
ANTONIO	Sure, it was a roar of a whole herd of lions!
ALONSO	Heard you this, Gonzalo?
GONZALO	Upon mine honour, sir, I heard a humming – there was a noise, that's verily.
ALONSO	Lead off this ground; and let's make further search for my poor son.

They all rise and leave the glade, watched by Ariel.

Another part of the island. Enter Caliban, bearing heavy logs for firewood on his back.

CALIBAN   All the infections that the sun sucks up from bogs, fens, flats, on Prosper fall, and make him by inch-meal, a disease . . .

Trinculo, the king's jester, who has also escaped the wreck enters. In his clown's motley, he presents a strange sight.

CALIBAN   Lo, now lo! Here comes a spirit of his, and to torment me for bringing wood in slowly. I'll fall flat; perchance he will not mind me!

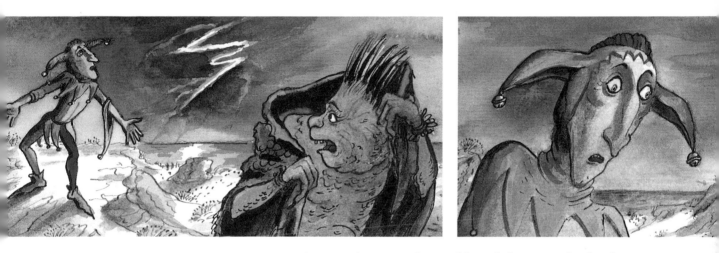

Caliban falls flat, and covers himself with his rough cloak. He lies motionless. Trinculo stumbles over him. Cautiously he investigates.

TRINCULO   What have we here? A man or a fish? Dead or alive? A fish: he smells like a fish; a very ancient and fish-like smell. (*He feels under the cloak.*) Warm, o'my troth! This is no fish, but an islander, who hath lately suffered by a thunder-bolt!

There is a loud peal of thunder.

Alas, the storm is come again! My best way is to creep under his gaberdine; there is no other shelter hereabout: misery acquaints a man with strange bed-fellows!

He creeps under the cloak and settles down, so that his legs and Caliban's protrude at opposite ends. Now comes yet another survivor. It is Stephano, the king's butler. As always he is clutching a bottle and is drunk. He sings.

STEPHANO

> I shall no more to sea, to sea
> Here shall I die ashore . . .

This is a very scurvy tune to sing at a man's funeral; here's my comfort!

He drinks, and kicks accidentally against the combined Caliban–Trinculo.

CALIBAN   Do not torment me—O!

Stephano investigates the four-legged cloak.

STEPHANO   This is some monster of the isle with four legs, who hath got, as I take it, an ague. Where the devil should he learn our language?

CALIBAN   Do not torment me, prithee; I'll bring my wood home faster.

STEPHANO   He is in his fit now, and does not talk after the wisest. He shall taste of my bottle. Come on your ways; open your mouth—

He thrusts the bottle under the cloak, and there is a noise of gulping.

TRINCULO   I should know that voice: it should be—but he is drowned!

STEPHANO   Four legs and two voices! Amen! I will pour some in thy other mouth!

TRINCULO   Stephano! If thou beest Stephano, touch me, and speak to me;
             for I am Trinculo!

STEPHANO   If thou beest Trinculo, come forth!

             *Trinculo comes forth. He and Stephano stare at one another;
             and then, in an access of joy, Trinculo seizes Stephano and
             whirls him round in a dance.*

TRINCULO   O Stephano, two Neapolitans 'scaped!

STEPHANO   Prithee, do not turn me about; my stomach is not constant.

CALIBAN   (*emerging*) That's a brave god, and bears celestial liquor. I will
             kneel to him.

STEPHANO   How didst thou 'scape? I escaped upon a butt of sack, which
             the sailors heaved o'erboard.

TRINCULO   O Stephano, hast any more of this?

STEPHANO   The whole butt, man.

CALIBAN   Hast thou not dropped from heaven?

             The two friends, as if for the first time, see Caliban kneeling.

STEPHANO   Out o'the moon, I do assure thee. I was the man i'the moon . . .

CALIBAN   I have seen thee in her, and I do adore thee!

STEPHANO	Come, swear to that; kiss the book. (*He proffers the bottle.*)
TRINCULO	This is a very shallow monster! The man i'th'moon! A most poor credulous monster!
CALIBAN	I will kiss thy foot; I prithee, be my god.
TRINCULO	I shall laugh myself to death at this puppy-headed monster! I could find in my heart to beat him—
STEPHANO	Come, kiss!
TRINCULO	—but that the poor monster's in drink!
CALIBAN	(*rising*) I'll show thee the best springs; I'll pluck thee berries; I'll fish for thee, and get thee wood enough. A plague upon the tyrant that I serve!
TRINCULO	A most ridiculous monster, to make a wonder of a poor drunkard!
STEPHANO	I prithee now, lead the way. Trinculo, the King and all our company else being drowned, we will inherit here!

Caliban takes up his burden of logs, and staggering drunkenly, leads the way and sings as he goes:

CALIBAN	'Ban, 'Ban, Cacaliban,
	Has a new master:—get a new man!
	Freedom, high-day! high-day, freedom!
	Freedom, high-day, freedom!

Before Prospero's cell. Ferdinand, a prisoner, staggers under the weight of a log that he bears from one pile to another. As he toils, Miranda slips out of the cell.

MIRANDA   Alas now, pray you, work not so hard. My father is hard at study; pray, now, rest yourself. He's safe for these three hours.

Prospero watches Miranda and Ferdinand from concealment. He smiles to himself.

PROSPERO   Poor worm, thou art infected.

MIRANDA   You look wearily.

FERDINAND   No, noble mistress: 'tis fresh morning with me when you are by at night. What is your name?

MIRANDA   Miranda.

FERDINAND   Admired Miranda! Indeed the top of admiration! Hear my soul speak: the very instant that I saw you, did my heart fly to your service!

MIRANDA   Do you love me?

FERDINAND   O heaven, O earth, bear witness! I, beyond all limit of what else i'th'world, do love, prize, honour you!

MIRANDA   I am a fool to weep at what I am glad of.

PROSPERO   Fair encounter of two most rare affections! Heavens rain grace on that which breeds between 'em!

FERDINAND   Wherefore weep you?

MIRANDA   At mine unworthiness, that dare not offer what I desire to give. I am your wife if you will marry me; if not, I'll die your maid.

FERDINAND   My mistress, dearest—

MIRANDA   My husband, then?

FERDINAND   Ay, with a heart as willing as bondage e'er of freedom. Here's my hand.

MIRANDA   And mine, with my heart in't. And now farewell till half an hour hence.

A forest clearing, in which Stephano has laid up his wine barrel. King-like, he sits upon it. Trinculo stands beside him, and Caliban lays his burden of firewood at his new master's feet. Stephano holds out his bottle.

STEPHANO   Servant-monster, drink to me!

TRINCULO   Servant-monster! The folly of this island! They say there's but five upon this isle: we are three of them; if th'other two be brain'd like us, the state totters.

CALIBAN   (*drinking*) How does thy honour? Let me lick thy shoe. I'll not serve him, he is not valiant.

TRINCULO   Thou liest, most ignorant monster!

STEPHANO   Trinculo, keep a good tongue in your head: if you prove a mutineer,—the next tree!

CALIBAN   I thank my noble lord. As I told thee before, I am subject to a tyrant, a sorcerer, that by his cunning hath cheated me of the island.

Ariel, as ever, invisible to all, appears and stands behind Trinculo.

ARIEL   (*in Trinculo's voice*) Thou liest!

CALIBAN   Thou liest, thou jesting monkey, thou! I would my valiant master would destroy thee, I do not lie.

STEPHANO   Trinculo, if you trouble him any more in's tale, by this hand, I will supplant some of your teeth!

TRINCULO   Why, I said nothing.

CALIBAN   I say, by sorcery he got this isle; from me he got it. If thy greatness will revenge it on him, thou shalt be lord of it, and I'll serve thee.

STEPHANO   How now shall this be compassed?

CALIBAN   I'll yield him to thee asleep, where thou mayst knock a nail into his head.

ARIEL   (*in Trinculo's voice*) Thou liest: thou canst not.

CALIBAN   What a pied ninny's this! Thou scurvy patch!

TRINCULO	Why, what did I? I did nothing.
ARIEL	(*in Trinculo's voice*) Thou liest.
STEPHANO	Take thou that! (*He beats Trinculo furiously. Trinculo retires in tears. Caliban claps his hands in delight.*) Now, forward with your tale.
CALIBAN	'Tis a custom with him in the afternoon to sleep: there thou mayst brain him having first seized his books. Remember, first to possess his books; for without them he's but a sot, as I am. Burn but his books. And that most deeply to consider is the beauty of his daughter; he himself calls her a nonpareil.
STEPHANO	Is it so brave a lass?
CALIBAN	Ay, lord, she will become thy bed, I warrant, and bring thee forth brave brood.
STEPHANO	Monster, I will kill this man: his daughter and I will be king and queen—save our graces!—and Trinculo and thyself shall be viceroys. Dost thou like the plot, Trinculo?
TRINCULO	Excellent!
STEPHANO	Give me thy hand, I am sorry I beat thee; but while thou liv'st, keep a good tongue in thy head.
CALIBAN	Within this half hour he will be asleep. Wilt thou destroy him then?
ARIEL	This will I tell my master. (*Ariel plays strange music.*)
TRINCULO	(*frightened*) O forgive me my sins!
STEPHANO	(*boldly*) He that dies pays all debts. I defy thee. Mercy upon us!

He strikes at the air, wildly, as the music seems to taunt them.

| CALIBAN | Be not afeared; the isle is full of noises, sounds and sweet airs, that give delight and hurt not. Sometimes a thousand twangling instruments will hum about mine ears; and sometimes voices, that if I then had waked after long sleep, will make me sleep again, and then in dreaming, the clouds methought would open, and show riches ready to drop upon me, that when I waked, I cried to dream again. |

STEPHANO   This will prove a brave kingdom to me, where I shall have my music for nothing.

CALIBAN   When Prospero is destroyed.

Another part of the island. The king and his followers are walking wearily through a wood.

GONZALO   By'r lakin, I can go no further, sir; my old bones ache.

ALONSO   Old lord, I cannot blame thee. Sit down and rest.

The king, Gonzalo and the attendant lords sit; Sebastian and Antonio draw apart.

SEBASTIAN   (*touching his sword*) The next advantage will we take thoroughly.

ANTONIO   Let it be tonight.

A strange, solemn music fills the air.

ANTONIO   What harmony is this?

GONZALO   Marvellous sweet music!

From concealment, Prospero watches his enemies. He raises his staff. Strange shapes, with beast and bird heads, appear, bearing a rich banquet. They set it down before the amazed company, bow, and vanish as suddenly as they had come.

ALONSO	Give us kind keepers, heavens! What were these?
SEBASTIAN	A living drollery.
GONZALO	If in Naples I should report this now, would they believe me?
ALONSO	I cannot too much muse such shapes, such gesture, and such sound expressing (although they want the use of tongue) a kind of excellent dumb discourse.
PROSPERO	(*to the apparitions*) Praise in departing.
GONZALO	They vanished strangely.
SEBASTIAN	No matter, since they have left their viands behind. Will't please you taste of what is here?

As they advance towards the table, there is thunder and lightning. The air darkens, and with a thudding of leathery wings, Ariel, in the form of a harpy, a hideous bird with the head of a hag, flies down and perches on the table. Prospero's enemies look on in astonishment when, at a clap of the bird's wings, the banquet vanishes.

ARIEL   (*screaming*) You are three men of sin—

All draw their swords and advance upon the apparition.

ARIEL   You fools! I and my fellows are ministers of Fate. Your swords are now too massy for your strengths.

Swords fall from helpless hands. The king and his company are motionless, spellbound.

ARIEL   You three from Milan did supplant good Prospero: exposed unto the sea him and his innocent child; for which foul deed the powers, delaying, not forgetting, have incensed the seas and shores, yea, all the creatures, against your peace. Thee of thy son, Alonso, they have bereft; and do pronounce by me ling'ring perdition . . .

Thunder and lightning; and Ariel vanishes.

THE TEMPEST

ALONSO O, it is monstrous, monstrous! Methought the billows spoke, and told me it, the winds did sing it to me, and the thunder, that deep and dreadful organ-pipe, pronounced the name of Prosper: therefore my son i'th'ooze is bedded; and I'll seek him deeper than e'er plummet sounded, and with him there lie mudded . . .

Before Prospero's cell, Ferdinand and Miranda together. Prospero smiles upon them. His harshness towards Ferdinand has vanished.

PROSPERO If I have too austerely punished you, your compensation makes amends. All thy vexations were but my trials of thy love, and thou hast strangely stood the test. Here, afore heaven, I ratify this, my rich gift. (*He gives Ferdinand Miranda's willing hand.*)

FERDINAND I do believe it, against an oracle.

PROSPERO Then, as my gift, and thine own acquisition, worthily purchased, take my daughter. Sit then and talk with her, she is thine own.

Prospero leaves the lovers to converse while he moves aside.

PROSPERO What Ariel! my industrious servant, Ariel!

ARIEL (*appearing*) What would my potent master?

PROSPERO   Go bring the rabble (o'er whom I give thee power) here to this place. Incite them to quick motion, for I must bestow upon the eyes of this young couple some vanity of mine art. It is my promise, and they expect it from me. (*Ariel departs on Prospero's errand. Prospero returns to Ferdinand and Miranda, who are embracing. Prospero shakes his head warningly.*)

PROSPERO   Do not give dalliance too much the rein.

FERDINAND   (*guiltily freeing Miranda*) I warrant you, sir—

PROSPERO   —No tongue! all eyes! Be silent!

Prospero raises his staff. Music plays and the air grows strangely bright, and full of swirling shapes. Iris, goddess of the rainbow appears, and, bowing, ushers in two goddesses more: Ceres, goddess of the harvest, and Juno, the queen of heaven.

JUNO   Honour, riches, marriage-blessing,
            Long continuance and increasing,
            Hourly joys be still upon you,
            Juno sings her blessings on you.

CERES   Earth's increase, foison plenty,
            Barns and garners never empty,
            Scarcity and want shall shun you,
            Ceres' blessing so is on you.

FERDINAND   (*awed*) This is a most majestic vision! May I be bold to think these spirits?

PROSPERO   Spirits which, by mine art, I have from their confines called to enact my present fancies.

More spirits appear, and dance gracefully.

FERDINAND   Let me live here ever! So rare a wondered father and a wise makes this place Paradise.

Prospero smiles. Suddenly his brow darkens.

PROSPERO   I had forgot that foul conspiracy of Caliban and his confederates against my life. The minute of their plot is almost come. Well done! Avoid! No more!

He gestures with his staff. The music jangles into discord and the spirits that have presented the marvellous vision fly, as if in terror. Ferdinand and Miranda look frightened.

PROSPERO   You do look, my son, in a moved sort, as if you were dismayed; be cheerful, sir. Our revels now are ended. These our actors (as I foretold you) were all spirits, and are melted into air, into thin air, and like the baseless fabric of this vision, the cloud clapped towers, the gorgeous palaces, the solemn

temples, the great globe itself, yea, all which it inherit, shall dissolve, and like this insubstantial pageant faded leave not a rack behind. We are such stuff as dreams are made on; and our little life is rounded with a sleep. Sir, I am vexed; bear with my weakness. If you be pleased, retire into my cell. A turn or two I'll walk to still my beating mind.

The lovers retire into Prospero's cell.

PROSPERO   Ariel, come!

ARIEL   (*appearing*) What's thy pleasure?

PROSPERO   Spirit, we must prepare to meet with Caliban. Where didst thou leave these varlots?

ARIEL   They were red-hot with drinking, so full of valour that they smote the air for breathing in their faces! I left them i'th'filthy-mantled pool beyond your cell, there dancing up to th'chins, that the foul lake o'erstunk their feet!

PROSPERO   This was well done, my bird. The trumpery in my house, go bring it hither, for stale to catch these thieves! (*Ariel departs.*) I will plague them all, even to roaring.

Ariel returns, bearing a host of rich garments, which, on Prospero's direction, are hung on a line close by the entrance to his cell. Then Prospero and Ariel conceal themselves. Even as they do so, the conspirators enter: Caliban, Stephano and Trinculo. They are soaked with filthy water.

CALIBAN	Pray you tread softly; we now are near his cell.
TRINCULO	Monster, I do smell all horse-piss, at which my nose is in great indignation.
STEPHANO	So is mine. Do you hear, monster?
CALIBAN	Prithee, my king, be quiet. Seest thou here, this is the mouth o'th'cell. No noise, and enter.
STEPHANO	Give me thy hand. I do begin to have bloody thoughts.
	Suddenly Trinculo sees the garments on the line.
TRINCULO	O King Stephano! Look what a wardrobe is here for thee!

THE TEMPEST

At once, the two drunkards busy themselves with all the fine clothing.

CALIBAN   Let it alone, thou fool, it is but trash!

STEPHANO   (*covetously*) Put off that gown, Trinculo. By this hand, I'll have that gown!

He tears the coveted garment off Trinculo.

CALIBAN   Let it alone, and do the murder first!

STEPHANO   Monster, go to, carry this!

He thrusts an armful of garments on Caliban.

TRINCULO   And this. (*More garments.*)

STEPHANO   Ay, and this!

Prospero raises his staff. At once, there is a sound of hunting horns, and out of the wood come huge, savage hounds, baying and barking. The would-be murderers howl in terror and dismay. They fly from the hounds. Prospero and Ariel urge the hunt on.

PROSPERO   Hey, Mountain, hey!

ARIEL   Silver! There goes Silver!

PROSPERO   Fury, Fury! There, Tyrant there! Hark, hark!

The sounds of barking and the howls of the pursued die away.

PROSPERO   Say, my spirit, how fares the King and's followers?

ARIEL   Just as you left them—all prisoners, sir. They cannot budge till your release. Your charm so strongly works 'em that if you now beheld them your affections would become tender.

PROSPERO   Dost think so, spirit?

ARIEL   Mine would, sir, were I human.

PROSPERO   And mine shall. The rarer action is in virtue than in vengeance. Go release them, Ariel.

Ariel departs. Prospero draws a circle on the ground with his staff. Sadly, he shakes his head.

PROSPERO   This rough magic I here abjure; and when I have required some heavenly music (which even now I do) to work mine end upon their senses that this airy charm is for, I'll break my staff, bury it certain fathoms in the earth, and deeper than did ever plummet sound I'll drown my book.

There is solemn music; Ariel leads the spellbound king and his followers into Prospero's magic circle, and leaves them, stiff and doll-like. Prospero now takes off his magic mantle and reveals the stately dress of the Duke of Milan. He waves his staff. The spell is lifted, and the prisoners blink in amazement.

PROSPERO   Behold, sir King, the wronged Duke of Milan, Prospero.

Alonso falls to his knees.

ALONSO	Thy dukedom I resign, and do entreat thou pardon me my wrongs. But how should Prospero be living, and be here?
PROSPERO	(*to Gonzalo*) First, noble friend, let me embrace thine age, whose honour cannot be measured or confined.
GONZALO	Whether this be, or be not, I'll not swear.
PROSPERO	You do yet taste some subtleties o' the isle, that will not let you believe things certain. Welcome, my friends all! (*He turns to Sebastian and Antonio.*) But you, my brace of lords, were I so minded, I here could pluck his Highness' frown upon you and justify you traitors. At this time I will tell no tales.
SEBASTIAN	(*aside*) The devil speaks in him!
PROSPERO	No. For you, most wicked sir, whom to call brother would even infect my mouth, I do forgive thy rankest fault—all of them; and require my dukedom of thee, which perforce, I know thou must restore.

Antonio scowls and shrugs his shoulders. He turns away. Prospero addresses the king.

PROSPERO	This cell's my court. Pray you, look in. My dukedom since you have given me again, I will requite you with as good a thing.

They approach the entrance to the cell. Prospero draws aside a curtain, and reveals Ferdinand and Miranda, playing chess.

MIRANDA   Sweet lord, you play me false.

FERDINAND   No, my dearest love, I would not for the world.

MIRANDA   Yes, for a score of kingdoms you should wrangle, and I would call it fair play—

The lovers, seeing they are observed, break off. Ferdinand runs to kneel at his father's feet.

FERDINAND   Though the seas threaten, they are merciful. I have cursed them without cause!

ALONSO   (*embracing him*) All the blessings of a glad father compass thee about!

MIRANDA   O, wonder! How many goodly creatures are there here! How beauteous mankind is! O brave new world, that has such people in it!

PROSPERO   'Tis new to thee.

ALONSO	Who is this maid with whom thou wast at play? Is she the goddess that hath severed us, and brought us together?
FERDINAND	Sir, she is mortal; but by immortal Providence she's mine. She is daughter to this famous Duke of Milan.

The king warmly embraces his son and his son's bride. Ariel enters, leading the ship's master and the boatswain, both in a state of dreamlike wonderment.

GONZALO	O look sir, look sir, here is more of us! What is the news?
BOATSWAIN	The best news is that we have safely found our king and company; the next, our ship—which but three glasses since, we gave out split—is tight and yare and bravely rigged as when we first put out to sea!
ARIEL	(*aside to Prospero*) Was't well done?
PROSPERO	Bravely, my diligence. Thou shalt be free. (*Ariel soars into the air and disappears.*)
ALONSO	This is as strange a maze as e'er men trod—

PROSPERO   There are yet missing of your company some few odd lads that
             you remember not. (*Ariel returns, driving a woeful Caliban
             and the reeling, drunken, tattered Stephano and Trinculo.*)
             Two of these fellows you must know and own. This thing of
             darkness I acknowledge mine. (*He turns to Caliban.*) Go,
             sirrah, to my cell. As you look to have my pardon, trim it
             handsomely.

CALIBAN   Ay, that I will; and I'll be wise hereafter, and seek for grace.
             What a thrice double ass was I to take this drunkard for a god,
             and worship this dull fool!

             *The three would-be lords of the isle stumble away to nurse
             their bruises and ease their cramps.*

ALONSO   I long to hear the story of your life, which must take the ear
             strangely.

PROSPERO   I'll deliver all, and promise you calm seas . . . (*To Ariel, aside*)
             My Ariel, chick, that is thy charge. Then to the elements be
             free, and fare thou well.

Prospero raises his hand in farewell. Then, with a courteous gesture, he conducts the company into his cell. For a moment, he remains alone. Then he breaks his magic staff and casts it away. Then he goes into the cell.

High up in the air, Ariel sings:

> Where the bee sucks, there suck I,
> In a cowslip's bell I lie;
> There I couch when owls do cry.
> On the bat's back I do fly
> After summer merrily.
> Merrily, merrily shall I live now,
> Under the blossom that hangs on the bough.

The curtain falls on the vessel that carries the king and his company back to Naples, and Prospero back to his dukedom, leaving Caliban to seek grace on the island.